Color Me Delighted In Your Law

A Psalm 119 Coloring Book

Laura R. Brown

Color Me Delighted Copyright ©2016 by Laura R. Brown

All rights reserved. No part of this book may be reproduced, scanned, or distributed in any printed or electronic form without permission.

Scripture is taken from the New American Standard Bible unless otherwise noted.

First Edition: August 2016
Printed in the United States of America
ISBN: 978-1-941749-62-3
Drawings used by permission Cyndi Calhoun

4-P Publishing
Chattanooga, TN

This coloring book can be used as a personal prayer and devotional or as a small-group prayer prompts. Before coloring the page, take the time to read the verse prompts. As you are coloring, pray, silently or audibly. If used in a group, I suggest playing instrumental music and allowing some time for individuals to color a page and then begin corporate prayer. I have also included prayer journal pages with a prayer focus prompt for those who may need a little help getting started. You will also find blank pages after every prayer journal page that you can use to be creative and draw your own pictures. I pray this coloring book is a blessing to anyone who chooses to use it.

Do you want to go deeper? Look for *"Delighting in the Law of the Lord Psalm 119 DevArtJournal"*. If you are one who enjoys variety in your study time you will find this study to be engaging. It is a guided time of active observation, investigative research, personal application, creative stimulation, and creative prayerful consideration. The "DevArtJournal" is designed to captivate the reader's attention and motivate to action. If you've grown weary of the usual Bible study patterns, this book is for you.

Laura

What Others are saying about "Delighting in the Law of Lord- Psalm 119 DevArtJournal...

I consider it both and honor as well as a privilege to endorse this very fine study of Psalm 119. Within its pages you will find a study that is comprehensive, exhaustive, creative and most of all, interactive. The blessings of the text will come alive in a way never before experienced by each participant of the study as they become thoroughly immersed in a "line upon line, precept upon precept" guide to this wonderful passage of Psalm 119. I highly recommend this engaging study for any Pastor or Group Leader desiring to be able to lead their participants in being able to draw fully from this powerful text as it has been masterfully prepared by the author.

Bishop S. T. Davis, Sr.
Mt. Pleasant Missionary Baptist Church
Winston Salem, NC

Creator, innovator, teacher, minister, visionary and friend; these are all words used to describe Laura Brown, who singlehandedly, I believe, with this book, will change the way meditation, prayer, and journaling is "supposed" to be done! We study the Psalm to gain an understanding of history and an appreciation of worship. Thank God for "right-brained" individuals to have permission to "be"…to create…to be free! This book outlines a practical way to apply Psalm 119 to our modern lives by emphasizing how God is the same yesterday, today and forever. As a Licensed Professional Counselor and Teacher, as well as a Pastor, I appreciate how Laura has married scripture, education, and psychology to enhance the learning experience(s) of those who get a "little" distracted by traditional methods of studying. I urge you to "relax", "relate", "release", and as Laura has encouraged…get your crayons, colored pencils, and a mug of your favorite hot beverage. Open your heart, mind, and ears to what Holy Spirit releases unto you during this study. Enjoy!
Miranda Y. Pearson, LPC, NCC, BCC

About Laura

Laura Brown is the founder and coach of "Wells of Truth Peer-Based Bible Coaching Group, where she teaches students how to study the Bible by using various study techniques. She is also a speaker and teacher at The Empowerment Church where she also serves on the Leadership Team. She has created several home Bible study curriculums that she has used in small group studies in her home. She is the creator and coach of the Serious Writers' Accountability Team (S.W.A.T.) Camp which is a writing and publishing camp for aspiring authors. She is the author of *"Delighting in the Law of the Lord- Psalm 119 DevArtJournal"* and *"Color Me Delighted in the Law- Psalm 119 Coloring Book"*, which can be purchased on Amazon.com

She has a heart to motivate believers into becoming life-long students of the Bible by equipping them with tools and techniques to create a sense of awe and adventure when approaching their devotional and study time in the Word of God.

Laura is a native of Toledo, Ohio and now resides in Chattanooga, TN. She is married to Wayne Brown and they have three children and two grandchildren. Laura enjoys all things creative. Whether designing custom jewelry, coasters, ornaments or meals for family and friends, she relishes in adding her personal touch to her creations. One of her favorite pastimes is dreaming of travel ideas for her husband and her to share with their granddaughters known as Secret Pop Pop and Nanna adventures.

You can connect with Laura at:

coachlaurabrown@gmail.com or www.swatbookcamp.com

BLESSED ARE THOSE WHO KEEP HIS TESTIMONIES

Read Psalm 119:1-3

Prayer Focus: The blessing in keeping God's word...

I AM NOT ASHAMED

Read Psalm 119:4-6

Prayer Focus: Not being ashamed to keep God word...

I Will Praise You With Uprightness Of Heart

Read Psalm 119:7-8

Prayer Focus: Praise of God's word...

WITH MY WHOLE HEART I HAVE SOUGHT YOU

Read Psalm 119:9-10

Prayer Focus: The cleansing power of God's word...

Read Psalm 119:11-12

Prayer Focus: The indwelling word of God...

I WILL NOT FORGET YOUR WORD

Read Psalm 119:13-16

Prayer Focus: Keeping God's word in view...

Read Psalm 119:17-20

Prayer Focus: The revelatory power of God's word...

REVIVE ME ACCORDING TO YOUR WORD

Read Psalm 119:21-24

Prayer Focus: God's word is our divine counselor...

TEACH ME YOUR STATUTES

Read Psalm 119:25-29

Prayer Focus: God's reviving word...

ENLARGE MY HEART

Read Psalm 119:30-32

Prayer Focus: Choosing God's word...

REVIVE ME

Read Psalm 119:33-40

Prayer Focus: Longing for God's word...

I TRUST IN YOUR WORD

Read Psalm 119:41-45

Prayer Focus: Hope & confidence in God's word...

Read Psalm 119:46-50

Prayer Focus: Comfort in God's word...

YOUR WORD IS MY SONG

Read Psalm 119:51-56

Prayer Focus: The joy of keeping God's law...

Read Psalm 119:57-61

Prayer Focus: God's word is satisfying...

I Delight In Your Law

Read Psalm 119:62-70

Prayer Focus: The convicting & saving power of God's word ...

YOUR HANDS HAVE MADE ME

Read Psalm 119:71-77

Prayer Focus: The beauty of those who follow God...

Read Psalm 119:78-83

Prayer Focus: God's vindicating word...

YOUR FAITH ENDURES

Read Psalm 119:84-91

Prayer Focus: Remaining steadfast in God's word through trials...

YOU GIVE ME LIFE

Read Psalm 119:92-96

Prayer Focus: God's word gives eternal life...

YOU MAKE ME WISE

Read Psalm 119:97-104

Prayer Focus: The sweet wisdom of God's word...

LIGHT MY PATH

Read Psalm 119:105 -112

Prayer Focus: God's guiding word...

YOU ARE MY SHIELD

Read Psalm 119:113-120

Prayer Focus: Finding refuge in God's word...

I SEEK YOUR WORD

Read Psalm 119:121-128

Prayer Focus: Longing to taught by God's word...

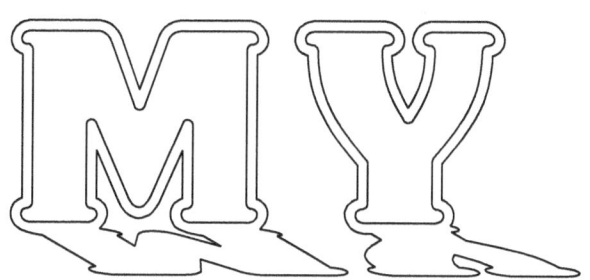

Read Psalm 119:129-136

Prayer Focus: Desire for everyone to love and follow God's law...

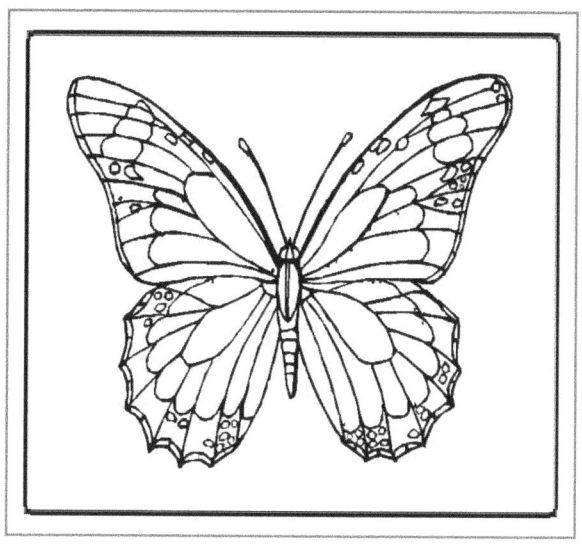

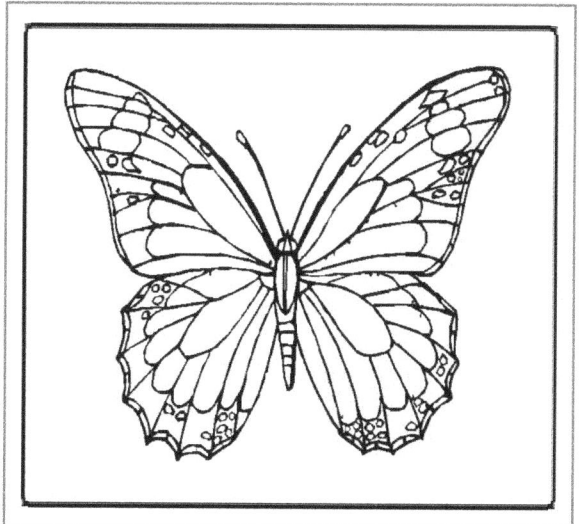

Read Psalm 119:137-144

Prayer Focus: Zeal for the pure word of God...

YOU ARE NEAR

Read Psalm 119:145-152

Prayer Focus: Word of God, speak to me...

Read Psalm 119:153-160

Prayer Focus: Deliver me from my affliction...

I STAND IN AWE OF YOU

Read Psalm 119:161-168

Prayer Focus: Peace and security in God's Word...

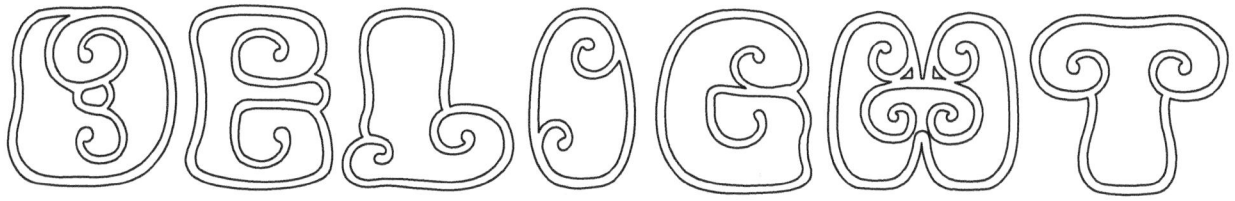

Read Psalm 119:169-176

Prayer Focus: Praising the righteous word of God...

www.ingramcontent.com/pod-product-compliance
Lightning Source LLC
Chambersburg PA
CBHW080940040426
42444CB00015B/3381